Natural Dyeing

Jackie Crook
with Geraldine Christy

LARK BOOKS

A Division of Sterling Publishing Co., Inc.
New York / London

Library of Congress Cataloging-in-Publication Data

Crook, Jackie, 1943-
      First ed.
            p. cm.
Natural Dyeing / Jackie Crook, with Geraldine Christy
      Includes index.
      ISBN-13: 978-1-60059-222-5 (pb-with flaps : alk. paper)
      ISBN-10: 1-60059-222-8 (pb-with flaps : alk. paper)
      1. Dyes and dyeing, Domestic. I. Christy, Geraldine. II. Title.
      TT854.3.C76 2007
      667'.3–dc22
2007011700

10 9 8 7 6 5 4 3 2 1

First Edition

Published by Lark Books, A Division of
Sterling Publishing Co., Inc.
387 Park Avenue South, New York, N.Y. 10016

First published 2007
Under the title NATURAL DYEING
By Gaia (an imprint, part of) Octopus Publishing Group Ltd
2–4 Heron Quays, Docklands, London E14 4JP

© 2007 Octopus Publishing Group Ltd
All rights reserved
Americanization © 2007 Octopus Publishing Group Ltd

Distributed in Canada by Sterling Publishing,
c/o Canadian Manda Group, 165 Dufferin Street
Toronto, Ontario, Canada M6K 3H6

If you have questions or comments about this book, please contact:
Lark Books
67 Broadway
Asheville, NC 28801
(828) 253-0467

Manufactured in China

ISBN 13: 978-1-60059-222-5
ISBN 10: 1-60059-222-8

For information about custom editions, special sales, premium and corporate purchases, please contact Sterling Special Sales Department at 800-805-5489 or specialsales@sterlingpub.com.

contents

introduction

Nature provides an abundance of plant materials that yield an infinite palette of luscious colors – from soft tints and pastels to vibrant mid tones and glowing deeps. The satisfaction of selecting natural dyes, such as roots, leaves, flowers and fruits as your source dyes, and the reward of seeing rich color taken up by yarns, fibers, fleeces and fabrics will inspire your creativity.

This book aims to teach you the easiest and simplest methods for natural dyeing in your own home. It will guide you through the whole process from start to finish with step-by-step instructions using tried and tested recipes. You do not need any specialized equipment and many of the required items are basic kitchenware. Although, it is important to remember to not use your dyeing equipment for cooking as some of the ingredients used to dye are toxic and many plants have poisonous parts.

You can dye any type of natural material – animal or vegetable – whether in the form of raw fibers or as fabric, threads or skeins. After thorough cleaning, most materials require treatment with a mordant, a chemical fixative that enables the take-up of dye. You can make decisive color changes with your choice of chemical ingredients.

This book describes three methods of dyeing, depending on the material. A hot water process works best for wool and cotton (see pages 23–25), but a cool water method is best for silk so as to maintain its natural sheen (see pages 26–28). If you wish to dye with indigo, for blue shades, you need a slightly different process known as vat dyeing (see pages 29–31).

Different fabrics and fibers take up dyes differently – no two batches are ever exactly the same color. This may be because of the particular qualities of the material – for instance, wool and silk are the easiest to use to achieve good colors. It may also be because the water you are using is more acid or alkaline, and of course, natural dyestuffs can vary in their dyeing ability. Despite the fact each dyeing session will produce different results, it is always a good idea to note down exactly the recipe and method you have used for future reference.

There are recipes for 30 projects in this book and examples are shown of five mordants for each of them – so you have 150 colors to start you off. But there are lots of other natural dyes – and lots of fun to be had in experimenting with your own sources and recipes.

how to use this book

Whether you are new to natural dyeing or you are an experienced dyer, this book is planned to help you produce beautiful colored fabrics and fibers. It sets out all the preparation and dyeing techniques you need in easy-to-follow steps, and then suggests 30 projects that will allow you to put them into practice right away.

The How to Dye chapter begins with an explanation of the necessary equipment and important advice on safety (see pages 8–9). With this information on board you can start to follow the techniques that are all described in methodical order of use.

The initial process in dyeing is to clean the cotton, silk or wool materials, and pages 10–13 explain how to do this. Next, pages 14–21 describe the role of mordants in fixing dye and how to use them, with a table of recommended quantities. Page 22 explains the three methods of dyeing – hot water, cool water and vat dyeing – and how to prepare the material for this stage. Pages 23–31 give detailed steps on how to make a dye bath and the process for each method. In all instructions throughout this book fibers are referred to generally as materials – wool, silk or cotton – unless otherwise stated. So you can choose the process you require for the type of material you are using.

The main part of the book consists of project recipes for specific dyestuffs and materials. Each recipe is for a specific material, and all techniques and projects are based on 3½ oz (100 g) material and 6–8 pints (3½–4½ litres) water. If you want to dye greater quantities of materials, simply increase all recipe quantities by the same proportion.

A mordanting process often takes place before dyeing a material to help the take-up (absorption) of dye. It also enables you to create a wider range of colors. A wool swatch is included with each project to show you the effect the addition of mordants can have on a material – there is also a color chart showing each of the dyestuffs with different mordants on pages 106–107.

In addition, a quick reference table that gives a summary of the best material to use for each natural dye can be found on pages 106–107; a glossary of terms is on pages 108–109; and throughout the book, there are tip boxes that highlight extra snippets of useful information.

how to dye

Dyeing involves several processes – preparing the material by cleaning, providing a mordant or fixative so that the dye will adhere to the material, and adding a coloring agent. The final coloring procedure takes place in two stages – making a liquid dye bath and immersing the material into the dye bath.

Tip The kitchen stove is an adequate heat source as long as you adhere to health and safety precautions (see page 9).

equipment

You need very little equipment to start dyeing, and all the items are ordinary kitchenware utensils. Any cooking vessel, including a large pan that is big enough to allow the free movement of material in water, is fine – stainless steel is a neutral material for pure colors, but aluminium pans will do. You can use your dye pan for both mordanting and dyeing.

Some kind of heat source is essential – a camping stove or portable electric ring is useful. You will also need a steel rod or knitting needle to stir dyestuffs and to immerse the material in the dye bath. Depending on the type of dyestuff used, you may also need a sieve and jelly bags, muslin or coffee filters to strain or filter plant material and powder residue out of the dye liquid, which you can decant into a large bowl. For those dyes that need to be made into a paste, have handy small glass bottles or jars.

Only a few natural dyes, such as madder, require specific temperatures to ensure the best results. For these dyes you will need a thermometer.

Keep your hands stain-free by wearing rubber gloves and protect your clothes with a waterproof apron and your workspace with plastic sheeting. Some natural dyes are toxic, so safety is very important (see page 9). Use a dust mask when working with powder dyes.

You will need
Large pan
Steel rod or knitting needle
Tongs
Rubber gloves
Dust mask
Waterproof apron
Weighing scales
Thermometer
Sieve
Jelly bags, muslin or coffee filters
Scales
Plastic sheeting
Heat source
Large bowl
Glass jar

Left from top left: saucepan and wooden tongs; glass bowl and stirring rods; sieve and weighing scales; dyepan, stirring rod, gloves and thermometer; small glass jars; measuring jugs.
Below: dust mask.

safety and disposal

Many plants have poisonous parts and, similarly, powdered dyestuffs, mordants, assistants and modifiers can also be harmful to health if ingested. Take care when handling all substances used in dyeing.

Use separate equipment for dyeing, reserving it solely for that purpose – it is not worth the risk of contaminating kitchen utensils with any residue from dyeing. Remember, too, that you are dealing with hot, sometimes boiling, liquids, which can scald and burn if tipped over. Also, be aware that large pans full of liquid can be very heavy.

Wear rubber gloves to protect your skin and a dust mask to avoid inhaling powders or fumes. Always dye in a well-ventilated area – outside is best, or perhaps in a shed, garage or workshop. If you have to work in the kitchen try to steer clear of areas used for food preparation. Cover work surfaces and clear up any drips and spills of dye liquid and substances

immediately. Always wipe down the surfaces well after you have finished a dyeing session and make sure you store the equipment used to dye with away from your food cooking equipment.

Keep your mordants and assistants in labelled containers for safety and easy recognition when making up a dye recipe, and make sure that they are out of reach of children and animals.

Dispose of dyeing substances responsibly. Toxic substances – particularly chrome, tin, copper and rhubarb leaf – should be emptied on waste ground, such as a gravel path, away from any drains or a watercourse. Non-toxic dye liquids and mordants may be emptied down the drain.

preparing materials for dyeing

All fibers and fabrics need to be thoroughly clean and free of grease before dyeing so that they take up the mordant and dye color evenly. The dressing applied to commercial yarns and fabrics also needs to be removed. This preparation of materials involves gentle washing and adequate rinsing.

ANIMAL AND VEGETABLE FIBERS

Any natural fibers or fabrics, animal or vegetable, can be used for dyeing. Wash wool by soaking for a short time in hot soapy water and prepare silk by soaking in warm soapy water for 30 minutes before rinsing thoroughly. Simmer vegetable fibers, such as cotton, slowly in a mild mixture of washing liquid and washing soda. With all fibers you may need to rinse more than once to make sure that the material is completely clean.

The following list categorizes some of the different types of wool, silk and cotton fibers and fabrics you can dye.

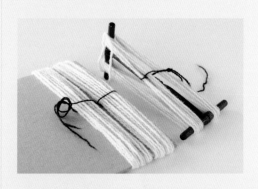

 Tip Wind yarn into hanks around a piece of cardboard (above left), a niddy noddy (above right), or a hank winder. Divide the yarn threads into two separate bunches and tie securely in four different places with some scrap yarn using a loose figure eight. Several small hanks are easier to manage than one large one, even for the same dye bath.

Wool
Raw fleece
Prepared unspun wool
Handspun wool
Unbleached wool yarn, commercially spun
Knitting wool
Tapestry wool
Felt (contains some synthetic fiber)

Silk
100 percent pure silk
Silk waste (de-gummed)
Unspun silk fibers
Silk yarn
Silk fabric

Cotton
100 percent pure cotton
Raw cotton
Cotton yarns – dishcloth, knitting and embroidery
Cotton fabric

CLEANING WOOL

Wool, whether yarn or fleece, contains natural oils and tiny particles of dirt. Once thoroughly cleaned and rinsed, wool fibers will take up mordant and dye easily and quickly, achieving good color results. Handle the wool with care when washing. As with other animal fibers, such as silk, put the material in the water in a large bowl or a dye pan; do not pour water directly onto the material.

1 Pour enough boiling water into a large glass bowl to allow the free movement of the material. Add 3 squirts of washing liquid.

2 Fully immerse the wool, gently pushing it under the water with a stirring rod. Do not agitate. Soak for 15 minutes.

3 Carefully remove the material. Rinse it in water that is the same temperature as the water from which the wool has just been removed. Repeat rinsing until the water is clear. Next, either hang out the wool to dry or mordant it for dyeing.

 Tip   Avoid felting by not agitating the wool in the water too much. Make sure that the temperatures of the washing and rinsing water do not vary greatly.

CLEANING SILK

Silk requires washing and dyeing at a low temperature to avoid damaging its surface and appearance. Like wool, silk receives natural dyes well. Colors on fine silk fabric look more vibrant than on the slightly nubbed texture of raw silk. It is best to use de-gummed silk, otherwise there will be a sticky residue that can be difficult to remove.

 Tip Never boil silk because extreme heat may destroy its natural characteristic sheen.

1 Prepare a warm water washing bath with plenty of water to cover the silk – no heat is necessary. Add 2 squirts of washing liquid to the water and agitate to ensure the soap is well dispersed.

2 Add the silk and allow it to soak for 30 minutes. This will help to release any impurities or grease. Agitate gently from time to time.

3 Remove and gently rinse the silk in warm water. Repeat rinsing until the water comes out clear. Next, either hang out the silk material to dry or mordant it for dyeing.

CLEANING COTTON

Cotton, a vegetable fiber, takes longer to prepare for dyeing than wool or silk. Wash cotton by simmering; in the course of doing so, various substances are released from the material into the water, causing a brownish discoloration. All cottons take color well if processed properly, but unbleached cotton may produce deeper shades.

 Put extra ties on hanks of cotton yarn (see page 10), as it can become very tangled during both the cleaning and dyeing process.

1 Add to the dye pan 2 teaspoons of washing soda, 3 squirts of washing liquid and the cotton fabric or fibers. Pour in enough warm water so the cotton is well covered. If necessary use a stirring rod to fully immerse the cotton.

2 Bring the water to simmering point and simmer for approximately 1 hour.

3 Carefully remove the cotton and rinse thoroughly in warm water, repeating until the water comes out clear – several changes of water may be required. Next, either hang out the cotton material to dry or mordant it for dyeing.

mordants

Mordants are minerals that are added to the material before dyeing. They react chemically with the dye and enable the prepared material to take up (absorb) the dye. They also improve the lightfastness and washfast properties of the color. Using different mordants can produce variations in color and shade – a wool swatch demonstrating the effect of mordants is included with each dye project.

TYPES OF MORDANTS
The mordants most commonly used are alum, chrome, copper, iron and tin. If you plan to do a lot of dyeing, it is useful to mordant a quantity of material at the same time. To identify the particular mordant used on a hank, tie knots at the ends. For example, you could use one knot to identify alum, two knots to identify chrome, three knots to identify copper, four for iron and five for tin. No knots could then mean no mordant was used.

ASSISTANTS
With some fibers an assistant is added to improve the absorption of the mordant into the material. These include cream of tartar, clear vinegar, tannic acid and washing soda (see page 15).

PREPARATION OF MATERIALS
Before both mordanting and dyeing it is important to wet the material thoroughly in warm water and a drop of washing liquid. Rinse thoroughly then squeeze out any excess water before you begin mordanting. This wetting of the material is because dry materials, especially cotton, float and don't take up liquid immediately, resulting in uneven mordanting and dyeing.

SAFETY
Because mordants are chemical substances wear rubber gloves and a dust mask when handling them. Dispose of residue mordant water responsibly, even though the quantities left in the dye bath after use are small. Chrome, tin and copper are hazardous chemicals, so empty these on waste ground, not down a drain or near a watercourse. Alum and iron are non-toxic chemicals, so very small amounts can be washed down the drain.

Above: Before mordanting all materials should be wet thoroughly and rinsed in warm water, then any excess water squeezed out.

MORDANT QUANTITIES

The amount of mordant required is a percentage of the dry weight of the material. For example, 3½ oz (100 g) material processed with 10 per cent mordant will need ⅓ oz (10 g) mordant.

Wool and silk

Mordant	Quantity	Assistants
Alum (potassium aluminium sulphate)	10 percent	7 percent cream of tartar
Chrome (potassium dichromate)	4 percent	None
Copper (copper sulphate)	5 percent	1 fl oz (30 ml) clear vinegar
Iron (ferrous sulphate)	3 percent	None
Tin (stannous chloride)	1 percent	2 percent cream of tartar

Cotton

Mordant	Quantity	Assistants
Alum (potassium aluminium sulphate)	20 percent	10 percent tannic acid 6 percent washing soda

Right: Madder-dyed wool yarns mordanted with iron, tin and chrome. Iron mordant (bottom left) usually darkens the dye shade; tin (bottom right) brightens the dye and tends to yellow the shade; chrome (top) tends to brown the dye shade.

MORDANTING WOOL

Wool absorbs mordants well and if you are using chrome and iron as your mordants you do not need to add an assistant. Alum is the mordant most commonly used for animal fibers as it helps achieve a clear, vivid color from the dye. If you are making up your own recipe follow the quantities given in the table on page 15. Each dyeing project in this book states the quantity of mordant required.

 Tip For safety-conscious dyers alum and iron mordants, which are non-toxic, give an adequate range of colors.

1 Dissolve the mordant in a little boiling water in a glass jar.

2 Fill a large pan (the dye bath) with sufficient warm water to allow free movement of the material, then add and stir in the mordanted water.

3 Add the wetted material and submerge using a stirring rod. Bring the water to simmering point and simmer for 1 hour. Occasionally move the material around gently with the rod to enable even uptake of the mordant.

4 Turn the heat off and leave the water and material to cool for 2–3 hours. For best results leave overnight.

5 Remove the material and rinse well in water that is the same temperature as the water from which the material has just been removed. Squeeze the material dry. You can now either hang out the material to completely dry or dye it.

MORDANTING SILK

Silk is processed for dyeing by using the same mordants as for wool. When mordanting silk, however, after the water reaches simmering point the heat is turned off and the liquid is then left to cool gently. Note that if too much iron is used as a mordant it can weaken animal fibers. Follow the quantities given in the table on page 15 if making up your own dye recipe. The quantity required to complete each of the dye projects is included with the recipe.

1 Dissolve the mordant in a little boiling water in a glass jar.

2 Fill a large pan (the dye bath) with enough warm water to allow free movement of the material, then stir in the mordanted water.

3 Add the wetted material and submerge it completely using a stirring rod. Heat the mordant bath to simmering point.

4 Carefully take the pan off the heat and allow the mordanted water and material to cool overnight.

 Tip Alum mordant gives a good range of lively colors on silk and will not affect the quality and luster of the material. For this reason alum is the best mordant to use on silk.

5 Remove the material, rinse well in cool water and squeeze out all excess water. You can now either dry or dye the material.

Tip Alum with tannic acid is the most commonly used mordant on cotton as an alum-mordanted material encourages a good dye take-up. Copper and tannic acid also may be used, but iron tends to darken materials too much.

MORDANTING COTTON

Vegetable fibers contain cellulose and require an extra stage to prepare them for mordanting. Soak cotton in water with tannic acid first to improve the absorption of alum into the fibers. Then use washing soda to act as an assistant in the mordanting process. Follow the quantities given in the table on page 15.

1 Dissolve the tannic acid in a little boiling water in a glass jar, then add it to a large saucepan of hot water.

2 Add the wetted material and submerge it using a stirring rod. Leave the material to stand in the water for 24 hours.

4 Dissolve the alum and washing soda in boiling water in a glass jar. Add this to a pan of fresh, hot water. Stir well to ensure the mordant is evenly dispersed.

3 Remove the material and rinse it well in cool water. You may want to rinse the material several times to ensure any residual tannic acid is removed from the cotton.

5 Now add the rinsed material, making sure it is fully submerged. Allow it to steep in the mordanted water for 24 hours, then remove the material and rinse thoroughly in cool water. You can now either dry or dye the mordanted material.

dyeing

There are three main methods of dyeing. Use hot water dyeing for wool and cotton, but you should only use cool water dyeing for silk so that its natural sheen is not damaged. Indigo dyestuff requires an additional stage to change its chemical content, so use the vat dyeing method to dye with indigo.

Wet the material before dyeing to ensure a better take-up of color. Dye the required quantity of material in one batch as it is virtually impossible to reproduce a color exactly. You can dye different types of well-rinsed mordanted material in one dye bath without the mordant leaching (changing the color of the other mordanted yarns). It is normal to use at least an equal weight of plant material to dry weight of material — more exact amounts are given in the recipes for each project. To change the depth of color you will find that more or less dyestuff will usually give darker and lighter shades.

Powdered dyes and powdered concentrated extracts are different commodities. The latter is a much stronger dye, so you need a smaller quantity if you are using it.

modifiers

You can make color changes to dyed fabrics and fibers by gently heating the dyed and rinsed material for five minutes in one of the following modifier solutions. Then rinse it again before drying. Note, however, that the color may not remain true if the dyed material is washed in a liquid with a different pH level to the pH of the modifier, either more acidic or more alkaline.

The effect of modifiers varies with the original plant material used, but generally an alkaline modifier (washing soda) shifts the dye shade towards blue; an acidic modifier (vinegar) shifts the dye towards red; and an iron modifier darkens or dulls the dye color.

Clear vinegar: 1 tsp per ½ pint (250 ml) water
Washing soda: 1 tsp per ½ pint (250 ml) water
Iron: ¼ tsp per ½ pint (250 ml) water

Red cabbage, alum and washing soda modifier

Red cabbage, alum and iron modifier

Red cabbage and alum

Red cabbage, alum and clear vinegar modifier

HOT WATER DYEING

The preparation of the dyestuff is the same for both hot water and cool water dyeing. After simmering leave the liquid dye to stand to develop its full strength. Straining the liquid before adding it to the dye bath ensures that no pieces of plant material or undissolved powder can affect the evenness of the dye when the material is processed in it. In hot water dyeing heat the material in the dyeing liquid at a constant simmer to avoid felting. In this example, weld tops have been used.

1 Break or cut up the plant material and place the small pieces of natural dye in a dye pan. Pour over enough boiling water to cover the dye material. If you are using powdered concentrated extract mix it to a paste with warm water and add this to the water in the pan.

2 Bring to a simmer and leave for about 1 hour. Top up with more boiling water if necessary.

3 Remove the dye pan from the heat and leave to steep for 1 hour, then strain or filter the liquid into a bowl.

4 Return the liquid dye to the dye pan and add the mordanted material. If the material is not still wet from being mordanted it will need to be wetted first – wring out any excess liquid. Add enough warm water so the material is fully immersed and to allow for free movement of the material. Stir two or three times.

 Tip You can re-use the reheated dye bath for further dips or 'exhausts' with more mordanted and wetted material. The resulting dye colors will become successively paler.

5 Bring the water to simmering point and simmer for 1 hour. Remove the dye pan from the heat. Leave to cool or until you obtain the depth of color you require. To check this, lift a section of the material out of the water using a stirring rod or tongs.

6 Once the dye bath is cool, remove the material and rinse in water. Continue until the rinse water is clear. Squeeze dry, then hang out the material to dry.

 Tip When rinsing dyed wool use water that is similar in temperature to the cooled dye bath to avoid felting.

COOL WATER DYEING

Always use this method when dyeing silk. The procedure is the same as for hot water dyeing except the material is not simmered in the dye bath – a high temperature will spoil the natural luster and will cause wrinkles in the fabric that are difficult to remove. Silk obtains a deep color much more quickly than either wool or cotton, in that order. Thin silk will dye a paler shade than thick silk from the same dye bath. In this example, Brazilwood has been used.

Tip Hard dyestuffs, such as bark or wood chips, need to be steeped at least overnight after simmering and before you strain them.

1 Break or cut up the plant material into small pieces and place the natural dye in a dye pan.

2 Pour over enough boiling water to cover the dye. If you are using powdered concentrated extract mix it to a paste with warm water and add this to the water in the pan. Bring to a simmer and leave for about 1 hour. Top up with more boiling water if necessary.

4 Return the liquid dye to the dye pan and add the mordanted material. If the material is not still wet from being mordanted it will need to be wetted first. Add enough warm water so the material is fully immersed and to allow for free movement of the material. Stir two or three times. Heat the water to just below simmering point, then remove the dye pan from the heat and allow the liquid to cool, or until the depth of color required is obtained.

3 Remove the dye pan from the heat and leave to steep for 1 hour, then strain or filter the liquid into a large bowl or saucepan.

5 Once the dye bath is cool, remove the material from the pan and rinse in water of a similar temperature to the cooled liquid. Continue until the rinse water is clear. Squeeze dry, then hang out the material to air dry.

 Tip While it is most common to use only hot water dying for wool and cotton it is not always necessary, as some dyes will color these materials using cool water dyeing – for example, annatto, madder and weld. Experiment with others. Remember, however, that heat often reveals the true color of the dye and improves lightfastness and washfastness.

VAT DYEING

This dyeing technique is slightly more involved than hot water dying and is used when dyeing with indigo as a dyestuff. It is definitely well worth the effort as vat dyeing is the only technique that will ensure a true blue dye. The shades of color achieved will range from pale blue to navy, depending on how long you leave the material in the dye pan. Refer to the dye project on pages 98–99 for the exact recipe to dye with indigo powdered concentrated extract.

1 Put the indigo powder in a small glass container. Gradually add drops of warm water, stirring between each addition, until a thin paste is obtained. Next add approximately ½ pint (250 ml) of warm water and stir well.

2 In a separate small container dissolve the washing soda in a small amount of boiling water, then add the mixture to the water in the dye pan.

3 Heat the liquid to 125°F (50°C) but no higher as this will destroy the dye color. Add the indigo dye liquid and stir well. Remove the pan from the heat and leave to stand for 30 minutes.

4 Reheat the dye bath to 125°F (50°C), then remove it from the heat and sprinkle the color run remover over the water's surface. Do not stir. Leave for 30 to 40 minutes.

Tip To obtain a true green, such as the color of grass or leaves, dye the material using a strong yellow natural dye, for example weld or goldenrod, then over-dye using indigo dyestuff. It is important to leave the yellow dyed material in the vat (step 5) for only 2–3 minutes or the blue will be too strong to produce green. If the green is not strong enough dip the yellow material in the indigo dye bath again.

5 Now carefully immerse the wetted material and leave it to stand. For darker shades of blue leave the material in the dye bath for approximately 20 minutes. Reduce this time for lighter shades of blue.

30

6 Remove the material quickly and carefully so as not to drip water back into the dye bath – you can re-use the dye bath, but introducing air to the dye through drips will eventually destroy the dye color.

7 Exposure to the air will immediately begin to change the color of the material to a deeper blue. Leave the material to air dry for 20 to 30 minutes, occasionally shaking gently to speed the airing process. Rinse, wash, rinse again and dry the dyed material.

roots

Hidden below ground, roots can provide
the dyer with unexpected color

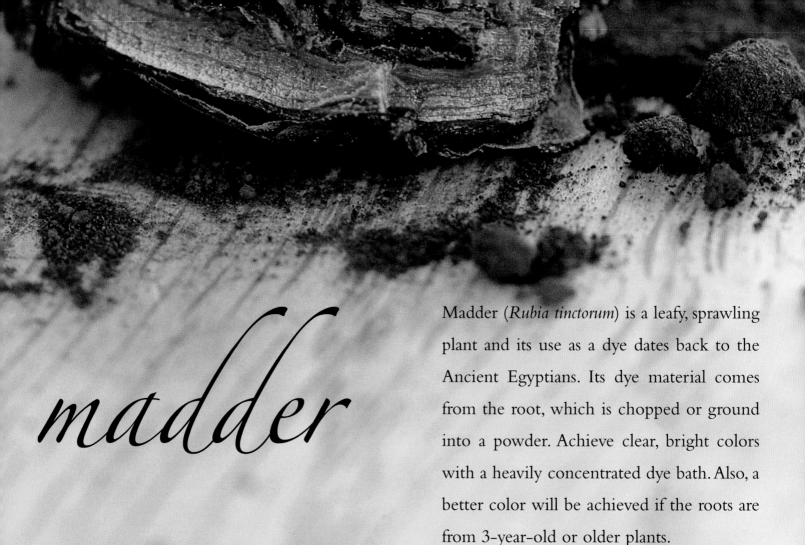

madder

Madder (*Rubia tinctorum*) is a leafy, sprawling plant and its use as a dye dates back to the Ancient Egyptians. Its dye material comes from the root, which is chopped or ground into a powder. Achieve clear, bright colors with a heavily concentrated dye bath. Also, a better color will be achieved if the roots are from 3-year-old or older plants.

You will need
3½ oz (100 g) silk fibers
¾ oz (20 g) madder powdered
   concentrated extract
6–8 pints (3½–4½ liters) water
Mordant used
Alum – ⅓ oz (10 g) plus ¼ oz (7 g)
   cream of tartar

Method
1 Use the cool water dyeing method as described on pages 26–28.
2 To make the dyebath simmer for 1–2 hours, until the dye is a deep mahogany hue.
3 Bring the silk fibers to a simmer, then leave the dye bath to cool until the fibers are the depth of pink or red you want.
4 Rinse the dyed silk fibers in warm water until the water comes out clear.

Tips For hot water dyeing with madder keep the water at 150°F (60°C) while the material is in the dye bath. Boiling will make the reds browner.

alum-mordanted silk fibers

mordanted wool yarns

alum-mordanted cotton yarn & fabric

Madder yields a rich range of colors, from pale pinks to earthy reds.

MORDANTED WOOL

Alum
Chrome
Copper
Iron
Tin

alkanet

Alkanet (*Alkanna tinctoria*) is a sprawling plant that grows in Europe. It is a member of the borage family and has small bright blue flowers, and hairy stems and leaves. The fresh roots of alkanet can give a reddish color that is used in cosmetics, but alcohol must be used to extract the pigment. For dyeing textiles the roots are dried and chopped, and produce a variety of soft tones.

You will need
3½ oz (100 g) silk fibers
3½ oz (100 g) dried alkanet root chips
6–8 pints (3½–4½ liters) water
Mordant used
Alum – ⅓ oz (10 g) plus ¼ oz (7 g) cream of tartar

Method
1 Use the cool water dyeing method as described on pages 26–28.
2 To make the dye bath simmer the dried alkanet root chips in water for 1 hour. Before straining, leave the dye mixture to steep for 1 hour.
3 Bring the silk fibers to a simmer in the dye bath, then leave to cool until the material is the color you require.
4 Rinse the dyed silk fibers in warm water.

 Tip Obtain grey shades on wool without a mordant, but use mordanted wool and hot water dyeing to produce lavenders and purple-greys.

alum-mordanted silk fibers & yarn

mordanted unspun wool

Alkanet gives heathery colors — purple-browns and mauve-greys.

MORDANTED WOOL

Alum

Chrome

Copper

Iron

Tin

37

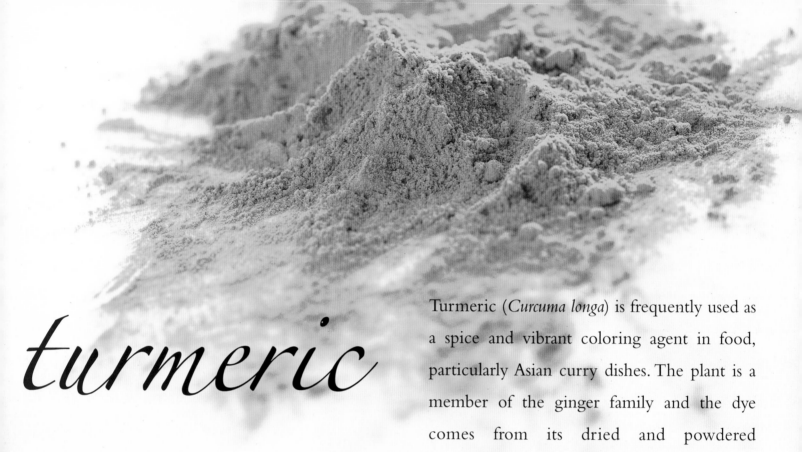

turmeric

Turmeric (*Curcuma longa*) is frequently used as a spice and vibrant coloring agent in food, particularly Asian curry dishes. The plant is a member of the ginger family and the dye comes from its dried and powdered underground stem or rhizome. Material dyed with turmeric is less lightfast than some other dyes and may fade in strong light.

You will need
3½ oz (100 g) unspun or double-knitting wool
1¾ oz (50 g) turmeric powder
6–8 pints (3½–4½ liters) water
Mordant used
Alum – ⅓ oz (10 g) plus ¼ oz (7 g) cream of tartar

Method
1 Use the hot water dyeing method as described on pages 23–25.
2 To make the dye bath make a paste with the turmeric powder and add it to the water. Simmer for 1 hour. Before filtering, leave the dye mixture to steep for 1 hour.
3 Bring the wool to a simmer in the dye bath, then simmer for 1 hour.
4 After simmering, leave the dye bath to cool until the wool is the shade of yellow you require.
5 Rinse the dyed wool in water that is similar in temperature to the cooled dye bath.

alum-mordanted unspun wool & wool yarn

Turmeric produces exotic golden yellows and warm, mid ochres.

Alum

Chrome

Copper

Iron

Tin

rhubarb

Rhubarb (*Rheum rhaponticum*) is a common kitchen-garden plant and its roots, fresh or dried as powder, are used as a dye for strong, deep colors. You can also use rhubarb leaves, which are poisonous and cannot be eaten, as a dye to produce paler yellow-green colors. There are several varieties of rhubarb, some of which may be used as a fixative or assistant to other dyes.

You will need

3½ oz (100 g) cotton fabric
1¾ oz (50 g) rhubarb root powder
6–8 pints (3½–4½ liters) water
Mordant used
Alum – ¾ oz (20 g) plus ⅓ oz (10 g) tannic acid and 6 g (⅕ oz) washing soda

Method

1 Use the hot water dyeing method as described on pages 23–25.
2 To make the dye bath make a paste with the rhubarb root powder and add it to the water. Simmer for 1 hour. Before filtering, leave the dye mixture to steep overnight.
3 Bring the cotton fabric to a simmer in the dye bath and continue to simmer for 1 hour.
4 After simmering, leave the dye bath to cool until the material is the depth of color you require.
5 Rinse the dyed cotton fabric in warm water until the water comes out clear.

Tip Simmer rhubarb leaves, which are poisonous, in water for 1 hour to yield oxalic acid. You can use this as a modifier to apply after dyeing a mordanted material to make the dyed color greener.

alum-mordanted cotton fabric

mordanted handspun wool

Rhubarb provides woodland tones from yellow to greenish bronze to copper.

MORDANTED WOOL

Alum

Chrome

Copper

Iron

Tin

41

woods
and barks

Trees — heartwood, branches and twigs — produce a warm, earthy palette

Brazilwood

Brazilwood (*Caesalpinia* species) is a traditional dye produced from the wood chips of the heartwood of a redwood tree. The dye has been used since medieval times in Europe and the discovery of Brazilwood growing as a native tree in South America led to the naming of the country Brazil. You can make successively paler pink colors by using the exhaust dye baths of brazilwood.

You will need

3½ oz (100 g) handspun or unspun wool
3½ oz (100 g) Brazilwood chips
6–8 pints (3½–4½ liters) water
Mordant used
Tin – ⅟₂₈ oz (1 g) plus ⅟₁₀ oz (2 g) cream of tartar

Method

1 Use the hot water dyeing method as described on pages 23–25.
2 To make the dye bath simmer the Brazilwood chips in water for 1 hour. Before straining, leave the dye mixture to steep overnight.
3 Bring the handspun or unspun wool to a simmer in the dye bath, then continue to simmer for 1 hour.
4 After simmering, leave the dye bath to cool until the wool is the color you require.
5 Rinse the dyed wool in water that is similar in temperature to the cooled dye bath.

Tips After dyeing the wood chips can be dried for further use. Clear vinegar as an assistant gives a more orange shade, while washing soda makes a 'bluer' red (see page 15).

Brazilwood gives delicious dark pinks, from raspberry through to blackberry.

tin-mordanted unspun & handspun wool

MORDANTED WOOL

Alum

Chrome

Copper

Iron

Tin

logwood

Logwood (*Haematoxylon campechianum*) trees grow in Central and South America, up to a height of 45 ft (13 m). The name dates from the 17th century when the wood was harvested and shipped to Europe. The dyestuff comes from the reddish heartwood of the tree. You can obtain beautiful purple shades from logwood, but they are not always lightfast or washfast. Some mordants are more successful than others.

You will need
3½ oz (100 g) silk fabric
1¾ oz (50 g) logwood chips
6–8 pints (3½–4½ liters) water
Mordant used
Alum – ⅓ oz (10 g) plus ¼ oz (7 g)
  cream of tartar

Method
1 Use the cool water dyeing method as described on pages 26–28.
2 To make the dye bath simmer the logwood chips in water for 1 hour. Before straining, leave the dye mixture to steep for 1 hour.
3 Bring the silk fabric to a simmer in the dye bath, then leave to cool until the material is the shade of mauve you require.
4 Rinse the dyed silk fabric in warm water.

Tips Purple obtained with an alum mordant on wool tends to fade, but an iron mordant or modifier increases fastness and gives deep purple to almost black colors. Dry the chips for further use.

alum-mordanted silk fabric

Logwood offers lovely colors from deep purple to soft mauves.

MORDANTED WOOL

Alum

Chrome

Copper

Iron

Tin

47

Cutch (*Acacia catechu*) is a small thorny tree that grows throughout the subcontinent of India. Its heartwood is rich in tannins and is used medicinally as well as for dyeing and tanning. Cutch is also known as black catechu and it was one of the original dyestuffs used to create a khaki-colored fabric for military uniforms. You can make successively paler colors by using the exhaust dye baths of cutch.

cutch

You will need
3½ oz (100 g) silk fabric
1¾ oz (50 g) cutch powder
6–8 pints (3½–4½ liters) water
Mordant used
Alum – ⅓ oz (10 g) plus ¼ oz (7 g)
   cream of tartar

Method
1 Use the cool water dyeing method as described on pages 26–28.
2 To make the dye bath make a paste with the cutch powder and add it to the water. Simmer for 1 hour. Before filtering, leave the dye mixture to steep for 1 hour.
3 Bring the silk fabric to a simmer in the dye bath, then leave to cool until the material is the color you require.
4 Rinse the dyed silk fabric in warm water.

Tip No mordant is necessary to obtain a yellow-brown and no heat is required if the material is soaked in a dye bath for several days. However, the resulting color is not very lightfast nor is it very washfast.

alum-mordanted silk fabric

mordanted unspun wool

Cutch yields a variety of orange-tans and biscuity browns.

MORDANTED WOOL

Alum

Chrome

Copper

Iron

Tin

buckthorn

Buckthorn (*Rhamnus* species) grows as a native evergreen bush in Europe and the Middle East and has become naturalized in areas of North America. There are several varieties of buckthorn and their use as dyestuffs dates back to at least medieval times. As well as its bark you can use the mature black berries of the shrub to produce a range of greenish yellow colors.

Tips The bark can be dried after use for future dyeing. Buckthorn berries (Persian berries) give yellow to green when using mordants and the hot water dyeing method.

You will need
3½ oz (100 g) silk fibers or yarn
1¾ oz (50 g) buckthorn wood chips
6–8 pints (3½–4½ liters) water
Mordant used
Alum – ⅓ oz (10 g) plus ¼ oz (7 g)
  cream of tartar

Method
1 Use the cool water dyeing method as described on pages 26–28.
2 To make the dye bath simmer the buckthorn wood chips in water for 1 hour. Before straining, leave the dye mixture to steep overnight.
3 Bring the silk fibers or yarn to a simmer in the dye bath, then leave to cool until the material is the colour you require.
4 Rinse the dyed silk fibers or yarn in warm water.

alum-mordanted silk fibers & yarns

mordanted unspun wool

Buckthorn gives rich honey, yellow, ginger and rust colors.

MORDANTED WOOL

Alum

Chrome

Copper

Iron

Tin

51

sanderswood

Sanderswood (*Pterocarpus santalinus*) is also known as red sandalwood. The tree grows in eastern regions of the Indian subcontinent, where it has been used as a dye for more than 3000 years. The heartwood of sanderswood contains a red dye, which is not soluble in water and a brown dye, which is released in hot water. As a dyestuff sanderswood is available as wood chips or as powder.

You will need

3½ oz (100 g) cotton fabric, fibers or yarn
3½ oz (100 g) sanderswood chips
6–8 pints (3½–4½ liters) water
Mordant used
Alum – ¾ oz (20 g) plus ⅓ oz (10 g) tannic acid and ⅕ oz (6 g) washing soda

Method

1 Use the hot water dyeing method as described on pages 23–25.
2 To make the dye bath simmer the sanderswood chips in water for 1 hour. Before straining, leave the dye mixture to steep for 1 hour.
3 Bring the cotton fabric, fibers or yarn to a simmer in the dye bath and continue to simmer for 1 hour.
4 After simmering, leave the dye bath to cool until the material is the color you require.
5 Rinse the dyed cotton material in warm water.

Tip You can often achieve stronger colors by leaving the dyestuff in the dye bath with the material. Strain the dyestuff and tie it securely in a muslin bag, then return this to the dye bath with the fibers. Stir from time to time for an even uptake of dye.

alum-mordanted cotton fabric, fibers & yarn

Sanderswood produces a range of pinkish browns and dark mushroom colors.

mordanted handspun wool yarns

MORDANTED WOOL

Alum

Chrome

Copper

Iron

Tin

osage orange

Osage orange (*Maclura pomifera*) is a tree that grows in North America, where it is also known as hedge apple. It bears large inedible orange fruits. The heartwood provides the dyestuff, as shavings, wood chips or as a concentrated powder. If you are using wood chips soak them overnight before starting the dyeing process to obtain a stronger dye. Dry them after use and re-use them for a lighter color.

You will need
3½ oz (100 g) silk fabric or yarn
⅕ oz (5 g) osage orange powdered concentrated extract
6–8 pints (3½–4½ liters) water
Mordant used
Alum – ⅓ oz (10 g) plus ¼ oz (7 g) cream of tartar

Method
1 Use the cool water dyeing method as described on pages 26–28.
2 To make the dye bath make a paste with the osage orange powdered concentrated extract and add it to the water in the dye bath. Simmer for 1 hour. Before filtering, leave the dye mixture to steep for 1 hour.
3 Bring the silk fabric or yarn to a simmer in the dye bath, then leave to cool until it is the shade of yellow you require.
4 Rinse the dyed fabric or yarn in warm water.

mordanted handspun wool yarns

alum-mordanted cotton yarn & fibers

alum-mordanted silk fabric & yarn

Osage orange yields yellows, mustards and ochres.

MORDANTED WOOL

Alum

Chrome

Copper

Iron

Tin

quebracho

Quebracho (*Quebrachea lorentzii*) is the name of several trees that grow in Paraguay that are rich in tannin. Their name comes from the Spanish for 'break axe', which is a reference to the hardness of the wood. Red quebracho provides a red dye that comes from both its bark and heartwood. It is used here for dyeing wool, but plant fibers such as cotton, linen and hemp also take up quebracho well.

You will need
3½ oz (100 g) unspun wool
1 oz (25 g) quebracho powdered concentrated extract
6–8 pints (3½–4½ liters) water
Mordant used
Tin – ⅟₂₈ oz (1 g) plus ⅟₁₀ oz (2 g) cream of tartar

Method
1 Use the hot water dyeing method as described on pages 23–25.
2 To make the dye bath make a paste with the quebracho powdered concentrated extract and add it to the dye bath. Simmer for 1 hour. Before filtering, leave the dye mixture to steep for 1 hour.
3 Bring the unspun wool to a simmer in the dye bath and continue to simmer for 1 hour.
4 After simmering, leave the dye bath to cool until the unspun wool is the color you require.
5 Rinse the dyed unspun wool in water that is similar in temperature to the cooled dye bath.

 Tip Browner shades are obtained on alum-mordanted wool, while silk tends to pick up dusty pink shades of color.

tin-mordanted unspun wool

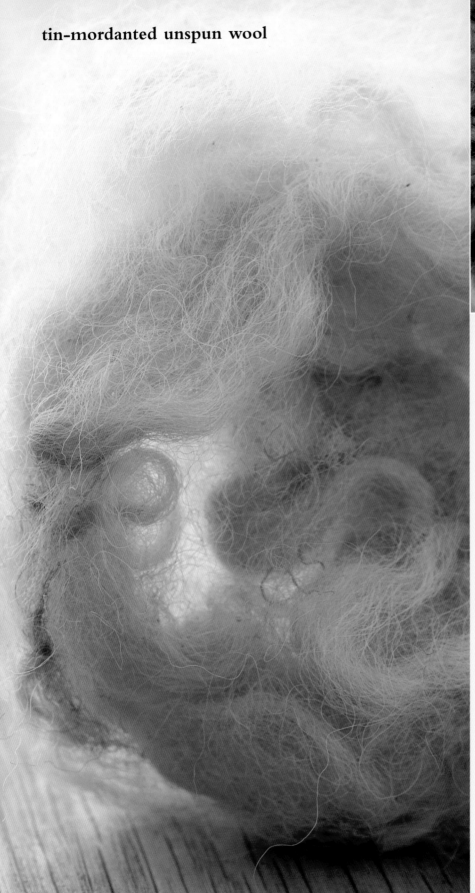

mordanted commercial
unbleached wool yarns

Quebracho gives rusty pinks and rose-browns, from peach to brick.

MORDANTED WOOL

Alum

Chrome

Copper

Iron

Tin

flowers

Flowers bring the summer sun,
giving yellows and oranges

gorse

Gorse (*Ulex europaeus*) is a shrub that grows widely on heathland throughout the British Isles and is also found in Australia and North America. It is a prickly bush that bears small bright yellow flowers that smell like coconut. The fresh flowers and gorse bark have long been used as dyestuffs, traditionally in Scotland for the coloring of wool to be woven into tartan.

You will need
3½ oz (100 g) unspun wool, wool yarn or felt fabric
3½ oz (100 g) fresh gorse flowers
6–8 pints (3½–4½ liters) water
Mordants used
Alum – ⅓ oz (10 g) plus ¼ oz (7 g) cream of tartar

Method
1 Use the hot water dyeing method as described on pages 23–25.
2 To make the dye bath simmer the fresh gorse flowers in water for 1 hour. Before straining, leave the dye mixture to steep for 1 hour.
3 Bring the unspun wool, wool yarn or felt fabric to a simmer in the dye bath and continue to simmer for 1 hour.
4 After simmering, leave the dye bath to cool until the material is the color you require.
5 Rinse the dyed material in water that is similar in temperature to the cooled dye bath.

Tip Flowering tops, including the gorse flowers, leaves and prickly stems, may be easier to use and will give a good color with all mordants.

alum-mordanted unspun wool, wool yarn & felt fabric

Gorse offers a range of earthy yellows and gold.

MORDANTED WOOL

Alum

Chrome

Copper

Iron

Tin

goldenrod

Goldenrod (*Solidago* species) is a leafy perennial garden plant that has clusters of tiny yellow flowers. It is a prolific native of North America and grows well in areas of Europe. You can use both flowers and leaves as a dyestuff, but the flower florets give the clearest colors. Crush them well in the dye bath to release the color. The fresher the flowers, the brighter the yellow dye will be.

You will need
3½ oz (100 g) silk fibers or yarn
3½ oz (100 g) fresh goldenrod flowers
6–8 pints (3½–4½ liters) water
Mordant used
Alum – ⅓ oz (10 g) plus ¼ oz (7 g) cream of tartar

Method
1 Use the cool water dyeing method as described on pages 26–28.
2 To make the dye bath simmer the fresh goldenrod flowers in water for 1 hour. Before straining, leave the dye mixture to steep for 1 hour.
3 Bring the silk fibers or yarn to a simmer in the dye bath, then leave to cool until the material is the shade of yellow you require.
4 Rinse the dyed silk fibers or yarn in warm water.

alum-mordanted silk yarn & fibers

mordanted commercial spun wool

Goldenrod produces yellows, from pale greenish tones to bright golds.

MORDANTED WOOL

Alum

Chrome

Copper

Iron

Tin

63

French marigold

French marigold (*Tagetes* species) is a small garden plant that originated in Central America, but now grows well in warm areas throughout the world. The dyestuff comes from the petals, which are characteristically bright orange but range from yellow to rust. Use fresh flowers or dried ones for dyeing. African marigolds are of the same species, but have larger blooms.

You will need
3½ oz (100 g) commercial unbleached wool
3½ oz (100 g) fresh French marigold flowers
6–8 pints (3½–4½ liters) water
Mordant used
Alum – ⅓ oz (10 g) plus ¼ oz (7 g) cream of tartar

Method
1 Use the hot water dyeing method as described on pages 23–25.
2 To make the dye bath simmer the fresh French marigold flowers in water for 1 hour. Before straining, leave the dye mixture to steep for 1 hour.
3 Bring the commercial unbleached wool to a simmer in the dye bath and continue to simmer for 1 hour.
4 After simmering, leave the dye bath to cool until the wool is the color you require.
5 Rinse the dyed wool in water that is similar in temperature to the cooled dye bath.

alum-mordanted commercial unbleached wool

mordanted unspun wool

French marigold gives mid yellows, from brownish to golden amber.

MORDANTED WOOL

Alum

Chrome

Copper

Iron

Tin

65

leaves
and stalks

The greenery of leaves and stalks offers a colorful, varied display

henna

Henna (*Lawsonia inermis*) is a shrub that grows in the hot, dry areas of Asia, the Middle East and North Africa. It is mostly known as a dye for hair and body decoration, particularly in India, but it produces good lightfast color when used to dye textiles. Henna's history as a dye goes back 5,000 years. The color comes from the leaves, which are dried and ground into a fine powder.

You will need
3½ oz (100 g) unspun wool
1¾ oz (50 g) henna powder
6–8 pints (3½–4½ liters) water
Mordant used
Chrome – ⅛ oz (4 g)

Method
1 Use the hot water dyeing method as described on pages 23–25.
2 To make the dye bath make a paste with the henna powder and add it to the water in the dye bath. Simmer for 1 hour. Before filtering, leave the dye mixture to steep for 1 hour.
3 Bring the unspun wool to a simmer in the dye bath and continue to simmer for 1 hour.
4 After simmering, leave the dye bath to cool until the wool is the color you require.
5 Rinse the dyed wool in water that is similar in temperature to the cooled dye bath.

Tip Iron is the only useful modifier to use with henna and produce shades of brown.

chrome-mordanted unspun wool

alum-mordanted cotton fabric & yarn

Henna gives a variety of pleasing yellow-browns and light rusts.

MORDANTED WOOL

Alum

Chrome

Copper

Iron

Tin

weld

Weld (*Reseda luteola*) was originally a European plant, and is also known as 'dyer's rocket'. Its history as a dyestuff dates back to the Romans. The source of the dye is its tops – flowers and leaves – which grow in the form of flowering spikes about 3 ft (1 m) in length. You can also use just the leaves. The color is very lightfast and washfast, and you can make lighter colors from successive exhaust dye baths.

You will need
3½ oz (100 g) muslin fabric
3½ oz (100 g) dried weld tops
6–8 pints (3½–4½ liters) water
Mordant used
Alum ¾ oz (20 g) plus ⅓ oz (10 g) tannic acid and ⅕ oz (6 g) washing soda

Method
1 Use the hot water dyeing method as described on pages 23–25.
2 To make the dye bath simmer the dried weld tops in water for 1 hour. Before straining, leave the dye mixture to steep for 1 hour.
3 Bring the muslin fabric to a simmer in the dye bath and continue to simmer for 1 hour.
4 After simmering, leave the dye bath to cool until the material is the shade of yellow you require.
5 Rinse the dyed muslin fabric in warm water.

Tip Weld gives a strong acid yellow with alum. This is a good base for over-dyeing with indigo to give a bright leaf green.

alum-mordanted muslin fabric

*Weld yields pale greens,
as well as bright yellows
and mustards.*

MORDANTED WOOL

Alum

Chrome

Copper

Iron

Tin

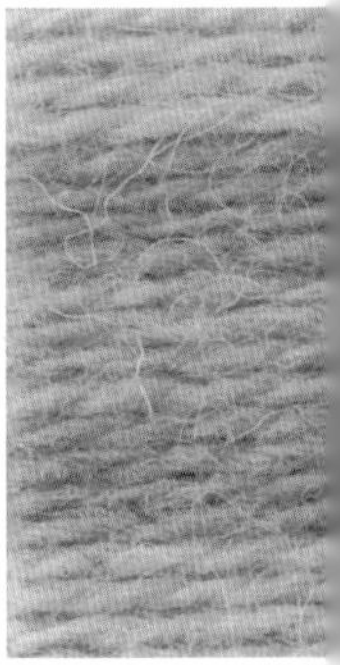

tea

Tea (*Thea sinensis*) is one of the most readily available dyestuffs. You have no need to buy specialist powder, but simply use the dried leaves that you keep in your kitchen cupboard to make a pot of tea. Split tea bags are just as useful. Tea contains tannin, which stains and colors, so material dyed with tea has good lightfast properties. Try this recipe, and then experiment with different strengths of tea.

You will need
3½ oz (100 g) handspun wool
3½ oz (100 g) black tea leaves
6–8 pints (3½–4½ liters) water
Mordant used
Copper – ⅕ oz (5 g) plus 1 fl oz (30 ml) clear
  vinegar

Method
1 Use the hot water dyeing method as described on pages 23–25.
2 To make the dye bath simmer the black tea leaves in water for 1 hour. Before straining, leave the dye mixture to steep for 1 hour.
3 Bring the handspun wool to a simmer in the dye bath and continue to simmer for 1 hour.
4 After simmering, leave the dye bath to cool until the wool is the color you require.
5 Rinse the dyed wool in water that is similar in temperature to the cooled dye bath.

Tip If you are dyeing with used tea leaves increase the proportion of leaves to material weight by at least half.

copper-mordanted handspun wool yarn
& alum-mordanted felt

alum-mordanted silk fabric, yarn
& unspun fibers

mordanted unspun wool

Tea creates a palette of warm browns, tans and rusts.

MORDANTED WOOL

Alum

Chrome

Copper

Iron

Tin

stinging nettle

Stinging nettle (*Urtica dioica*) is a weed found commonly in many places throughout the world and the young tops are often used as a leafy vegetable in Europe. Gather both leaves and stalks as fresh as possible to give clear, bright colors in the dye bath. You can also dry them to use later for brownish tones. Remember to wear gloves to protect your hands when working with nettles!

You will need
3½ oz (100 g) silk yarn or fabric
3½ oz (100 g) fresh stinging nettle leaves and stalks
6–8 pints (3½–4½ liters) water
Mordant used
Alum – ⅓ oz (10 g) plus ¼ oz (7 g) cream of tartar

Method
1 Use the cool water dyeing method as described on pages 26–28.
2 To make the dye bath simmer the chopped stinging nettle leaves and stalks in water for 1 hour. Leave the dye mixture to steep for 1 hour before straining.
3 Bring the silk yarn or fabric to a simmer in the dye bath, then leave to cool until the material is the color you require.
4 Rinse the dyed silk yarn or fabric in warm water.

alum-mordanted silk yarn & fabric

mordanted wool yarns

Stinging nettle produces greens and yellows, from pale to deep.

Alum

Chrome

Copper

Iron

Tin

Tansy (*Tanacetum vulgare*) is a lovely wild flower or cottage plant, with clusters of bright yellow button flowers and mid green serrated leaves. It is an aromatic plant and was once popular as a summer fly repellent. Use the fresh flowers on their own as a dyestuff or combine them with the leaves and stalks. You can also dry the plant materials for later use.

tansy

You will need
3½ oz (100 g) handspun wool
3½ oz (100 g) fresh tansy leaves and stalks
6–8 pints (3½–4½ liters) water
Mordant used
Copper – ⅕ oz (5 g) plus 1 fl oz (30 ml) cream of tartar

Method
1 Use the hot water dyeing method as described on pages 23–25.
2 To make the dye bath simmer the fresh tansy leaves and stalks in water for 1 hour. Before straining, leave the dye mixture to steep for 1 hour.
3 Bring the handspun wool to a simmer in the dye bath and continue to simmer for 1 hour.
4 After simmering, leave the dye bath to cool until the wool is the color you require.
5 Rinse the dyed wool thoroughly in water that is similar in temperature to the cooled dye bath.

Tip Tansy is a good source of olive green when alum-mordanted dyed wool is modified with iron.

mordanted unspun wool

copper-mordanted handspun wool

Tansy gives fresh yellow-greens
with tinges of mustard and bronze.

MORDANTED WOOL

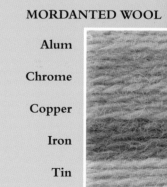

Alum

Chrome

Copper

Iron

Tin

77

fruits
and vegetables

Delicious fruits and vegetables
— a wealth of surprising hues

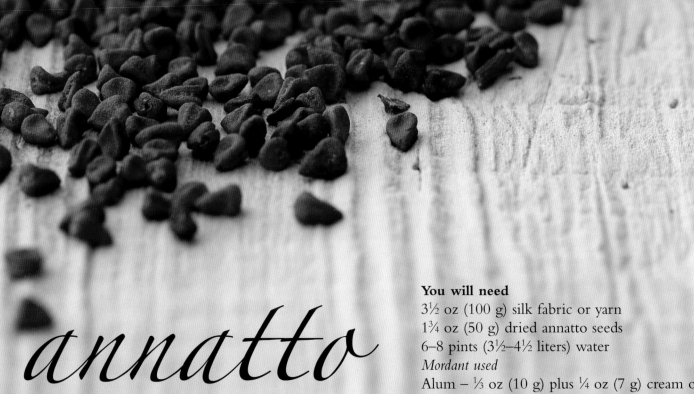

annatto

Annatto (*Bixa orellana*) is an evergreen shrub that originated in South and Central America and now grows in other tropical areas of the world. Its flowers develop into clusters of dark red seedpods, giving it the nickname 'lipstick tree'. The dyestuff comes from the red seeds, which are released when the pods are ripe. Annatto is a familiar food coloring, too, used in butter and cheese.

You will need
3½ oz (100 g) silk fabric or yarn
1¾ oz (50 g) dried annatto seeds
6–8 pints (3½–4½ liters) water
Mordant used
Alum – ⅓ oz (10 g) plus ¼ oz (7 g) cream of tartar

Method
1 Use the cool water dyeing method as described on pages 26–28.
2 To make the dye bath simmer the dried annatto seeds in water for 1 hour. Before straining, leave the dye mixture to steep for 1 hour.
3 Bring the silk fabric or yarn to a simmer in the dye bath, turn off the heat, then leave the material to cool until it is the shade of orange you require.
4 Rinse the dyed silk fabric or yarn in warm water.

Tip Obtain a yellow-apricot color with no mordant by adding a teaspoon of washing soda to the seeds when simmering them to produce the dye.

alum-mordanted silk fabric & yarn

mordanted wool yarns

Annatto gives glowing shades of red-orange, gold and apricot.

Elderberry or elder (*Sambucus* species) grows as a wild shrub or tree and is the subject of much country lore. Make cordial, wine or jam from the berries and flowers, and use all parts of the plant – berries, leaves or bark – as dyestuffs. Purple colors come from the berries, either fresh or dry. Elderberry dyes tend to fade, but the variety of colors you can obtain with modifiers makes them worth trying.

You will need

3½ oz (100 g) silk fabric or yarn
7 oz (200 g) dried elderberries
6–8 pints (3½–4½ liters) water
Mordant used
Alum – ⅓ oz (10 g) plus ¼ oz (7 g) cream
   of tartar

Method

1 Use the cool water dyeing method as described on pages 26–28.
2 To make the dye bath simmer the dried elderberries in water for 1 hour. Before straining, leave the dye mixture to steep for 1 hour.
3 Bring the silk fabric or yarn to a simmer in the dye bath, then leave to cool until the material is the color you require.
4 Rinse the dyed silk fabric or yarn in warm water.

elderberry

Tips Elderberry, like most purple fruit dyes, is good for showing the effect of different modifiers (see page 22). Clear vinegar reddens the color, washing soda gives greens, and iron blackens the color. Elderberry is fun to use, but the colors are not very lightfast or washfast.

Elderberry makes soft colors – pale purple-greys and lichen greens.

alum-mordanted silk fabric & yarn

MORDANTED WOOL

Alum

Chrome

Copper

Iron

Tin

83

walnut

Walnut (*Juglans nigra*) is a tree that is native to North America and gives the richest color, though you can also use other species of walnut for dyeing. You can use all parts of the tree for dyeing, but the richest browns come from the husks. If you are using dried husks – which yield much paler, fawn shades – use a quantity of husks that is equal to the material weight.

Tip No mordant is necessary to achieve good color with fresh husks, but if you use dried dyestuff you will find that mordanted wool gives better color.

You will need
3½ oz (100 g) unspun wool
1¾ oz (50 g) dried green walnut husks
6–8 pints (3½–4½ liters) water
Mordant used
No mordant required

Method
1 Use the hot water dyeing method as described on pages 23–25.
2 To make the dye bath simmer the dried green walnut husks in water for 1 hour. Before straining, leave the dye mixture to steep for 1 hour.
3 Bring the unspun wool to a simmer in the dye bath and continue to simmer for 1 hour.
4 After simmering, leave the dye bath to cool until the wool is the color you require.
5 Rinse the dyed wool in water that is similar in temperature to the cooled dye bath.

unmordanted silk fabric & fibers

unmordanted cotton yarn & fibers

unmordanted unspun wool

*Walnut yields rich,
peaty tones of brown and chocolate.*

MORDANTED WOOL

Alum

Chrome

Copper

Iron

Tin

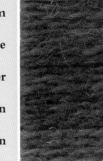

Blackberry (*Rubus fruticosus*) or bramble is a prolific hedgerow bush with prickly stems that is also cultivated in gardens. Its juicy berries provide food for man and beast, and are a good dyestuff. Pick the berries yourself if you can – sort through them well to remove any insects. Blackberry leaves and stems provide greyish tones, but they do not give the lovely purple colors of the berry juice.

blackberry

Tip Try using frozen blackberries when the fresh ones are out of season. You can still produce good shades on mordanted material.

You will need
3½ oz (100 g) unspun wool
10½ oz (300 g) fresh blackberries
6–8 pints (3½–4½ liters) water
Mordant used
Iron – ¹/₁₀ oz (3 g)

Method
1 Use the hot water dyeing method as described on pages 23–25.
2 To make the dye bath simmer the fresh black-berries in water for 1 hour. Before straining, leave the dye mixture to steep for 1 hour.
3 Bring the unspun wool to a simmer in the dye bath and continue to simmer for 1 hour.
4 After simmering, leave the dye bath to cool until the wool is the color you require.
5 Rinse the dyed wool in water that is similar in temperature to the cooled dye bath.

mordanted handspun wool

Blackberry yields a feast of delicious mauves, lilacs and purples.

MORDANTED WOOL

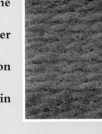

Alum

Chrome

Copper

Iron

Tin

iron-mordanted unspun wool

87

red cabbage

Red cabbage (*Brassica capitata*) is a readily available leafy vegetable. Its leaves contain a pigment known as anthocyanin, which is also found in beetroot and which leaches into water when you are cooking the vegetable. This natural coloring is used in foodstuffs and you can also use it to dye fibers and fabrics. Mordants generally have the effect of changing the dark red-purple dye to a range of soft blue-greens.

Tip Alum-mordanted yarn can be modified with obvious results – washing soda emphasizes the blue-green, vinegar reddens and iron darkens the original shade after dyeing.

You will need
3½ oz (100 g) silk fibers
7 oz (200 g) fresh red cabbage
6–8 pints (3½–4½ liters) water
Mordant used
Alum – ⅓ oz (10 g) plus ¼ oz (7 g)
  cream of tartar

Method
1 Use the cool water dyeing method as described on pages 26–28.
2 To make the dye bath simmer the fresh red cabbage in water for 1 hour. Before straining, leave the dye mixture to steep for 1 hour.
3 Bring the silk fibers to a simmer in the dye bath, then leave to cool until the material is the color you require.
4 Rinse the dyed silk fibers in warm water.

alum-mordanted silk fibers

mordanted felt &
wool yarns

Red cabbage produces
a varied array of
greens and mauve.

MORDANTED WOOL

Alum

Chrome

Copper

Iron

Tin

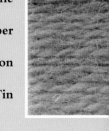

onion

Onion (*Allium cepa*) is an easy dyestuff to find – ask for the discarded skins at the bottom of storage crates at your local store. The color comes from the papery outer skins and varies depending on the type of onions you use – surprisingly, red onion skins produce a yellow color. You can over-dye material with indigo to produce different greens (see pages 98–99).

You will need
3½ oz (100 g) unspun wool
1¾ oz (50 g) dried, brown outer onion skins
6–8 pints (3½–4½ liters) water
Mordant used
Chrome – ⅛ oz (4 g)

Method
1 Use the hot water dyeing method as described on pages 23–25.
2 To make the dye bath simmer the dried onion skins in water for 1 hour. Before straining, leave the dye mixture to steep for 1 hour.
3 Bring the unspun wool to a simmer in the dye bath and continue to simmer for 1 hour.
4 After simmering, leave the dye bath to cool until the wool is the color you require.
5 Rinse the dyed wool in warm water.

 Tip You can use onion skins for dyeing without a mordant to produce good color. However, mordants increase the range of colors, all of which are strong, lightfast and washfast.

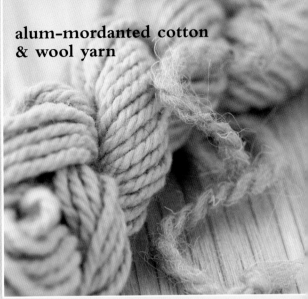

alum-mordanted cotton & wool yarn

Onion skins give rich, rusty oranges and golden browns.

chrome-mordanted unspun wool

MORDANTED WOOL

Alum

Chrome

Copper

Iron

Tin

avocado

Avocado (*Persea americana*) comes originally from Mexico and Central America, where it was discovered by the Spanish conquistadors and introduced to Europe. The tree grows to a height of 60 ft (20 m) and bears nutritious fleshy pear-shaped fruits, a staple food of the Aztecs. Use the avocado skin as a dyestuff, making sure that it is well washed, then dried.

You will need

3½ oz (100 g) unspun wool
7 oz (200 g) washed and dried avocado skins
6–8 pints (3½–4½ liters) water
Mordant used
Chrome – ⅛ oz (4 g)

Method

1 Use the hot water dyeing method as described on pages 23–25.
2 To make the dye bath simmer the dried avocado skins in water for 1 hour. Before straining, leave the dye mixture to steep for 1 hour.
3 Bring the unspun wool to a simmer in the dye bath and continue to simmer for 1 hour.
4 After simmering, leave the dye bath to cool until the wool is the color you require.
5 Rinse the dyed wool in water that is similar in temperature to the cooled dye bath.

Tip Wash and clean away any residue flesh inside the skin to prevent molding in the drying process.

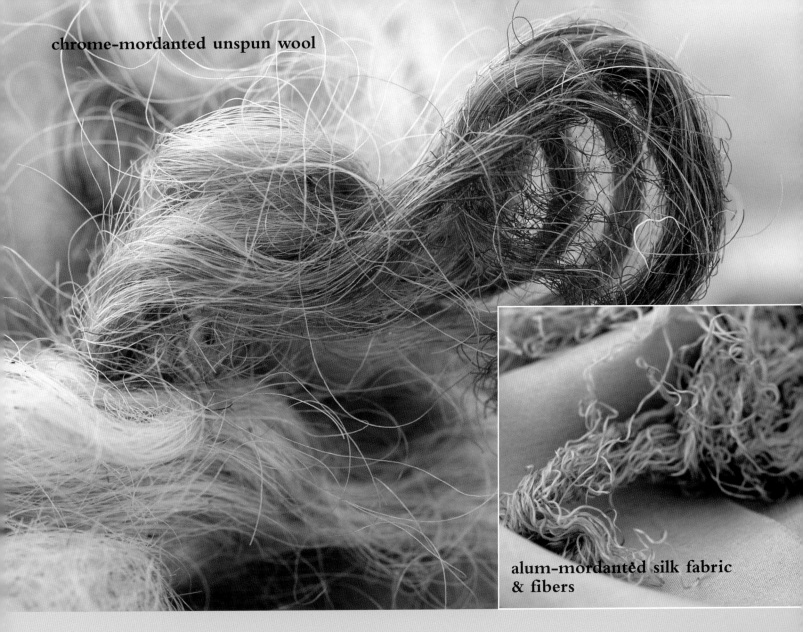

chrome-mordanted unspun wool

alum-mordanted silk fabric & fibers

Avocado skins yield an unusual range of coral and rose-browns.

MORDANTED WOOL

Alum

Chrome

Copper

Iron

Tin

ivy

Ivy (*Hedera helix*) is a hardy evergreen climbing plant. As a climber, ivy grows vigorously up and over walls, trees, fences and hedgerows, clinging on with the help of aerial roots. You can use the leaves for dyeing, but you will achieve brighter green colors if you use the berries. Gather the ripe black berries, which are poisonous, in the late autumn and use them fresh.

You will need

3½ oz (100 g) silk fibers, yarn or fabric
14 oz (400 g) fresh ivy berries
6–8 pints (3½–4½ liters) water
Mordant used
Alum – ⅓ oz (10 g) plus ¼ oz (7 g) cream of tartar

Method

1 Use the cool water dyeing method as described on pages 26–28.
2 To make the dye bath simmer the fresh ivy berries in water for 1 hour. Before straining, leave the dye mixture to steep for 1 hour.
3 Bring the silk fibers, yarn or fabric to a simmer in the dye bath, then leave to cool until the material is the color you require.
4 Rinse the dyed silk material in warm water.

Tip Ivy berries produce soft shades on all mordanted materials.

alum-mordanted silk fibers, yarn & fabric

**alum-mordanted cotton
yarn & fabric**

*Ivy berries produce
muted minty greens
and greenish-grey.*

MORDANTED WOOL

Alum

Chrome

Copper

Iron

Tin

95

special
colors

Exotic crimsons and pinks — and
indigo is the blue to dye for

Indigo (*Indigofera* species) is a shrub that grows in humid conditions throughout the world. The dye, which gives denim its blue color, is extracted from its leaves. Indigo requires a different method of dyeing – vat dyeing. The addition of washing soda ensures an alkaline liquid and the addition of a color run remover removes oxygen, leaving 'indigo white'. The material takes up the indigo white in the dye bath and turns blue when taken out and exposed to the oxygen in the air.

indigo

You will need
3½ oz (100 g) unspun wool
⅕ oz (5 g) indigo powdered concentrated extract
6–8 pints (3½–4½ liters) water
⅛ oz (4 g) washing soda
¾ oz (20 g) color run remover
Mordant used
No mordant required

Method
1 Use the vat dyeing method as described on pages 29–31.
2 Mix the indigo powdered concentrated extract to a thin paste, then mix into a solution by adding 1 pint (500 ml) of warm water.
3 To make the dye bath, add the washing soda mixture to the dye pan and heat the water to a maximum of 125°F (50°C), then add the indigo powder and water mixture to the heated water mixture. Leave to stand for 30 minutes.
4 After reheating the dye bath add the color run remover. Do not stir. Leave for 30–40 minutes.
5 Add the unspun wool. Leave for 20 minutes for dark shades, less for lighter blues.
6 Remove the wool quickly without letting it drip. Allow to air dry for 20–30 minutes.
7 Rinse the dyed wool in water that is similar in temperature to the cooled dye bath.

 Tip Because indigo is a vat dye no mordant is ever needed. The dye bath will continue to give progressively paler shades for several separate exhausts, but the material needs to be left in the dye bath for increasing amounts of time. For example, 2 or more hours for pale blues and greys.

unmordanted unspun wool

unmordanted silk fabric

Indigo offers every blue shade, from the palest sky to inky black.

UNMORDANTED WOOL

40 minutes

20 minutes

15 minutes

10 minutes

5 minutes

cochineal

Cochineal comes from a scale insect (*Dactylopius coccus*) that lives on a prickly pear cactus growing in Mexico and other parts of Central and South America. The color comes from a fluid stored by the insect as defense against predators and is extracted as a dyestuff from the dried husks of the animal. Cochineal was brought to Europe by the Spanish conquistadors in the 16th century. It is a very lightfast color.

You will need

3½ oz (100 g) handspun wool
⅒ oz (5 g) cochineal powdered concentrated extract
6–8 pints (3½–4½ liters) water
Mordant used
Tin – ⅟₂₈ oz (1 g) plus ⅒ oz (2 g) cream of tartar

Method

1 Use the hot water dyeing method as described on pages 23–25.
2 To make the dye bath make a paste with the cochineal powdered concentrated extract and add it to the water in the dye bath. Simmer for 1 hour. Before filtering, leave the dye mixture to steep for 1 hour.
3 Bring the handspun wool to a simmer in the dye bath and continue to simmer for 1 hour.
4 After simmering, leave the dye bath to cool until the wool is the shade of crimson you require.
5 Rinse the dyed wool in water that is similar in temperature to the cooled dye bath.

Tip Cochineal is sensitive to acids and minerals – for best results when dyeing use rainwater or distilled water.

tin-mordanted handspun wool

mordanted wool yarn & felt

Cochineal gives lovely rose-pinks, carmines and crimson-reds.

MORDANTED WOOL

Alum

Chrome

Copper

Iron

Tin

lac

Lac is a resin that is secreted by an insect (*Laccifer lacca*) on the branches of ficus trees in India and surrounding parts of Asia. The resin is dried, then powdered, to make a dyestuff. Lac was a valuable color that was much used commercially until the invention of aniline dyes in the 19th century. Lac provided the main red color in traditional Persian carpets.

You will need

3½ oz (100 g) silk fabric
¾ oz (20 g) lac powdered concentrated extract
6–8 pints (3½–4½ liters) water
Mordant used
Alum – ⅓ oz (10 g) plus ¼ oz (7 g) cream of tartar

Method

1 Use the cool water dyeing method as described on pages 26–28.
2 To make the dye bath make a paste with the lac powdered concentrated extract and add it to the water in the dye bath. Simmer for 1 hour. Before filtering, leave the dye mixture to steep for 1 hour.
3 Bring the silk fabric to a simmer in the dye bath, then leave to cool until the the material is the red you require.
4 Rinse the dyed silk fabric in warm water.

Tip For bluer purples over-dye lac red with indigo. Dip the material in the indigo vat for 2–3 minutes, then check the color. Repeat until you obtain the shade you require.

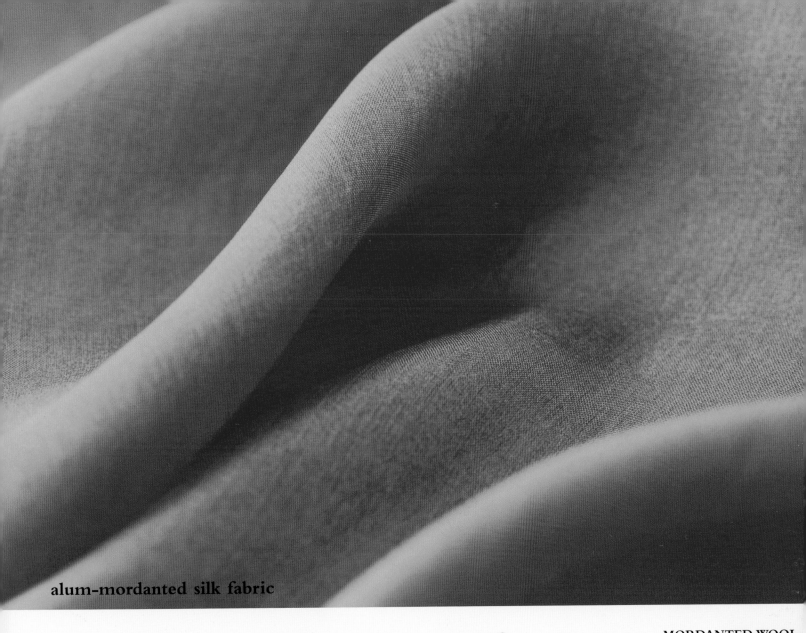

alum-mordanted silk fabric

Lac produces a range of purple-reds, burgundy and maroon.

Alum

Chrome

Copper

Iron

Tin

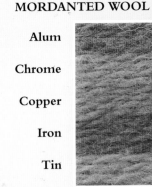

optimizing your natural dyes

Materials vary in the way they take up dye, and some dyestuffs give stronger color than others. This table provides a quick reference for the dyestuffs used in this book and suggests the best source of dye to use to extract the fullest strength of color. Dyestuffs are available in many forms including roots, wood chips or shavings, bark, berries, flowers, leaves, stalks, skins, seeds and plant tops, as fresh or dried substances, or as powdered concentrated extract.

Common name *Latin name*	Silk	Wool	Cotton	Dyestuff
Roots				
Madder *Rubia tinctorum*		✔		Fresh, dried root powder, powdered concentrated extract
Alkanet *Alkanna tinctoria*		✔		Dried roots
Turmeric *Curcuma longa*		✔		Powder
Rhubarb *Rheum rhaponticum*		✔		Fresh, powder
Wood and barks				
Brazilwood *Caesalpinia* species		✔		Wood chips
Logwood *Haematoxylon campechianum*	✔			Wood chips, powdered concentrated extract
Cutch *Acacia catechu*		✔		Powder
Buckthorn *Rhamnus species*	✔			Bark, dried berries
Sanderswood *Pterocarpus santalinus*		✔		Wood chips
Osage orange *Maclura pomifera*		✔		Powdered concentrated extract
Quebracho *Quebrachea lorentzii*	✔			Powdered concentrated extract

Common name *Latin name*	Silk	Wool	Cotton	Dyestuff
Flowers				
Gorse *Ulex europaeus*		✔		Fresh tops
Goldenrod *Solidago* species		✔		Fresh tops, dried tops
French marigold *Tagetes* species		✔		Fresh tops
Leaves and stalks				
Henna *Lawsonia inermis*		✔		Powder
Weld *Reseda luteola*		✔		Fresh tops, dried tops
Tea *Thea sinensis*		✔		Dried leaves, tea bags
Stinging nettle *Urtica dioica*		✔		Fresh tops
Tansy *Tanacetum vulgare*		✔		Fresh tops, dried tops
Fruits and vegetables				
Annatto *Bixa orellana*	✔	✔		Seeds
Elderberry *Sambucus* species	✔			Fresh berries, dried berries
Walnut *Juglans nigra*		✔		Fresh husks, dried husks
Blackberry *Rubus fruticosus*	✔			Fresh berries, frozen berries
Red cabbage *Brassica capitata*	✔			Fresh
Onion *Allium cepa*		✔		Dried outer skins
Avocado *Persea americana*		✔		Fresh skins home dried
Ivy *Hedera helix*		✔		Fresh berries
Special colors				
Indigo *Indigofera* species		✔		Powdered concentrated extract
Cochineal *Dactylopius coccus*		✔		Powdered concentrated extract, powder, dried insects
Lac *Laccifer lacca*	✔			Powdered concentrated extract, dried resin

color chart

These color swatches show the colors obtained on wool yarn by using the 30 dyestuffs in this book. Each of the swatches displays five effects by using five different mordants – alum, chrome, copper, iron and tin. Your own dyeing may produce slightly different colors depending on the acidity or alkalinity of the water you use, but these swatches show what a wonderful range of colors you can achieve.

Madder
(*Rubia tinctorum*)
(see pages 34–35)

Alkanet
(*Alkanna tinctoria*)
(see pages 36–37)

Turmeric
(*Curcuma longa*)
(see pages 38–39)

Rhubarb root
(*Rheum rhaponticum*)
(see pages 40–41)

Brazilwood
(*Caesalpinia* species)
(see pages 44–45)

Logwood
(*Haematoxylon campechianum*)
(see pages 46–47)

Cutch
(*Acacia catechu*)
(see pages 48–49)

Buckthorn
(*Rhamnus* species)
(see pages 50–51)

Sanderswood
(*Pterocarpus santalinus*)
(see pages 52–53)

Osage orange
(*Maclura pomifera*)
(see pages 54–55)

Quebracho
(*Quebrachea lorentzii*)
(see pages 56–57)

Gorse
(*Ulex europaeus*)
(see pages 60–61)

Goldenrod
(*Solidago* species)
(see pages 62–63)

French marigold
(*Tagetes* species)
(see pages 64–65)

Henna
(*Lawsonia inermis*)
(see pages 68–69)

Weld
(*Reseda luteola*)
(see pages 70–71)

Tea
(*Thea sinensis*)
(see pages 72–73)

Stinging nettle
(*Urtica dioica*)
(see pages 74–75)

Tansy
(*Tanacetum vulgare*)
(see pages 76–77)

Annatto
(*Bixa orellana*)
(see pages 80–81)

Elderberry
(*Sambucus* species)
(see pages 82–83)

Walnut
(*Juglans nigra*)
(see pages 84–85)

Blackberry
(*Rubus fruticosus*)
(see pages 86–87)

Red cabbage
(*Brassica capitata*)
(see pages 88–89)

Onion
(*Allium cepa*)
(see pages 90–91)

Avocado
(*Persea americana*)
(see pages 92–93)

Ivy
(*Hedera helix*)
(see pages 94–95)

Indigo
(*Indigofera* species)
(see pages 98–99)

Cochineal
(*Dactylopius coccus*)
(see pages 100–101)

Lac
(*Laccifer lacca*)
(see pages 102–103)

glossary

Alkanet A plant of the borage family, whose roots provide a purplish dye.

Alum A mineral used as a mordant or fixative in dyeing.

Aniline dye One of many synthetic dyes first developed in the 19th century.

Annatto A tropical shrub whose ripe red seeds give an orange dye.

Anthocyanin A natural blue-red pigment contained in vegetables such as red cabbage and beetroot.

Assistant An additive used with a mordant to improve absorption of the mordant into the material.

Avocado The skins of this Central American fruit yield a variety of brown colors.

Blackberry A hedgerow or garden fruit that gives a variety of light and deep purple shades.

Brazilwood The heartwood of this South American tree is used as a dye to give reds.

Buckthorn An evergreen bush, whose bark and berries give strong yellow dyes.

Chrome A mineral used as a mordant or fixative in dyeing.

Clear vinegar A liquid additive used as an assistant in the mordanting process and also as a modifier to change the colors of dyed material.

Cochineal A crimson-red dye that comes from cactus-living scale insects in Central and South America.

Cool dyeing A process used for dyeing silk.

Copper A mineral used as a mordant or fixative in dyeing.

Cream of tartar An additive used as an assistant in the mordanting process to help dye take-up.

Cutch An Asian tree whose heartwood gives yellow-browns.

Dressing A treatment of sealant or size glue used for stiffening fabrics.

Dye bath The liquid dye in which the material to be dyed is immersed to color it.

Dyestuff The source of a dye, whether roots, wood chips or shavings, bark, berries, flowers, leaves, stalks, skins, seeds and plant tops, as fresh or dried substances, or as powdered concentrated extract.

Elderberry A purple fruit that gives a wide range of purple to green colors when used with modifiers.

Exhausts The used dye-bath liquid that may be used for further dyeing.

Felting The matting together of wool fibers caused by agitation in hot water.

French marigold These easy-to-grow orange flowers give a range of yellow to amber colors.

Goldenrod The fresh or dried flowers of this garden plant produce a yellow dye.

Gorse A prickly shrub, whose flowers, bark and stems give yellow colors.

Hank Circular loops or coils of yarn tied securely to avoid tangling during the dye process and storage.

Henna The leaves of this Asian shrub are dried to produce a powder that gives brown shades for dyeing.

Hot water dyeing A process used for dyeing wool and cotton. Heat reveals the true color of the dye.

Indigo A blue dye extracted from this plant is produced by vat dyeing. Indigo provides the blue color for denim, and if over-dyed with bright yellow produces true greens such as grass or green leaves.

Iron A mineral used as both a mordant or fixative and as a modifier of color in dyeing.

Ivy The berries of this climbing evergreen plant produce soft green colors.

Lac Also known as sticklac, this dye is a resin secreted by insects that live on ficus trees in parts of Asia.

Leaching The loss of color when a material is wetted.

Lightfastness The ability of a dye not to fade when subjected to light over a period of time.

Logwood A South American tree whose heartwood produces bluish purple dyes.

Madder A sprawling plant whose roots produce a red dye, used since the time of the Ancient Egyptians.

Materials Natural animal and vegetable wools, cottons and silks used in the form of raw fibers or as fabric, threads or skeins.

Modifier A substance added to change the color of dyed material.

Mordant/Mordanting A mineral (usually alum, chrome, copper, iron or tin) that is diluted in water and used to pre-treat the material to enable the absorption of dye.

Onion The papery skins of white or red onions give a yellow-brown dye.

Osage orange A North American tree whose heartwood gives mustard-yellow colors.

pH level The scale by which the acidity or alkalinity of a liquid may be measured.

Quebracho A South American tree rich in tannin. Its heartwood and bark give a red dye.

Red cabbage A leafy vegetable that contains the natural red-blue pigment anthocyanin, which acts as a dye.

Rhubarb The root of this plant gives yellow to green colors.

Sanderswood An Asian tree whose heartwood gives an unusual pinkish brown dye color.

Skein See hank.

Stinging nettle The leaves and stems of this wayside weed produce green and yellow colors.

Tannic acid An additive used as an assistant in the mordanting process.

Tansy A wild or garden plant, whose yellow flowers, leaves and stalks produce yellow and green colors.

Tea A ready source of dye, tea leaves produce shades of brown colors.

Tin A mineral used as a mordant or fixative when dyeing materials.

Turmeric A plant whose underground stem gives a yellow dye. It is also used to spice and color food.

Vat dyeing The process of dyeing used specifically for coloring material with indigo.

Walnut A tree, whose nut husks, fresh or dried, give a range of warm brown colors.

Washfastness The ability of a dye to keep its color after washing.

Washing soda An additive used as an assistant in the mordanting process and also as a modifier to change the color of dyed material.

Weld A yellow flowering plant, whose tops produce yellow and green colors.

index

Acknowledgements

Editor **Camilla Davis**
Executive Art Editor **Leigh Jones**
Designer **Jo Tapper**
Photographer **Vanessa Davies**
Production Manager **Simone Nauerth**
Co-writer **Geraldine Christy**

Picture Acknowledgements
Special photography:
© Octopus Publishing Group Ltd/Vanessa Davies
Other photography:
Alamy/Jim Lane 54. **The Garden Collection**/Torie Chugg 64.
Octopus Publishing Group Ltd/Jerry Harpur 62; /Sandra Lane 90;
/William Lingwood 40, 86; /William Reavell 38; /Gareth Sambidge
88. **Leigh Jones** 82. **Nature Photographers Ltd**/Paul Sterry 74, 76.

Bibliography

Dean, J, *Wild Colour*, London, Mitchell Beazley, 1999
Goodwin, J, *A Dyer's Manual*, Hessle, UK, Ashman's Publications, 2003
Sugar, M, *The Complete Natural Dyeing Guide*, Lemoyne, PA, Rug
Hooking, 2002
Robertson, S, *Dyes from Plants*, New York, Van Nostrand Reinhold, 1973
Delamare, F and Guineau, B, *Colour: Making and Using Dyes and
Pigments*, London, Thames & Hudson, 2000